AF575508

ROAD ROLLERS

Paul Zachary

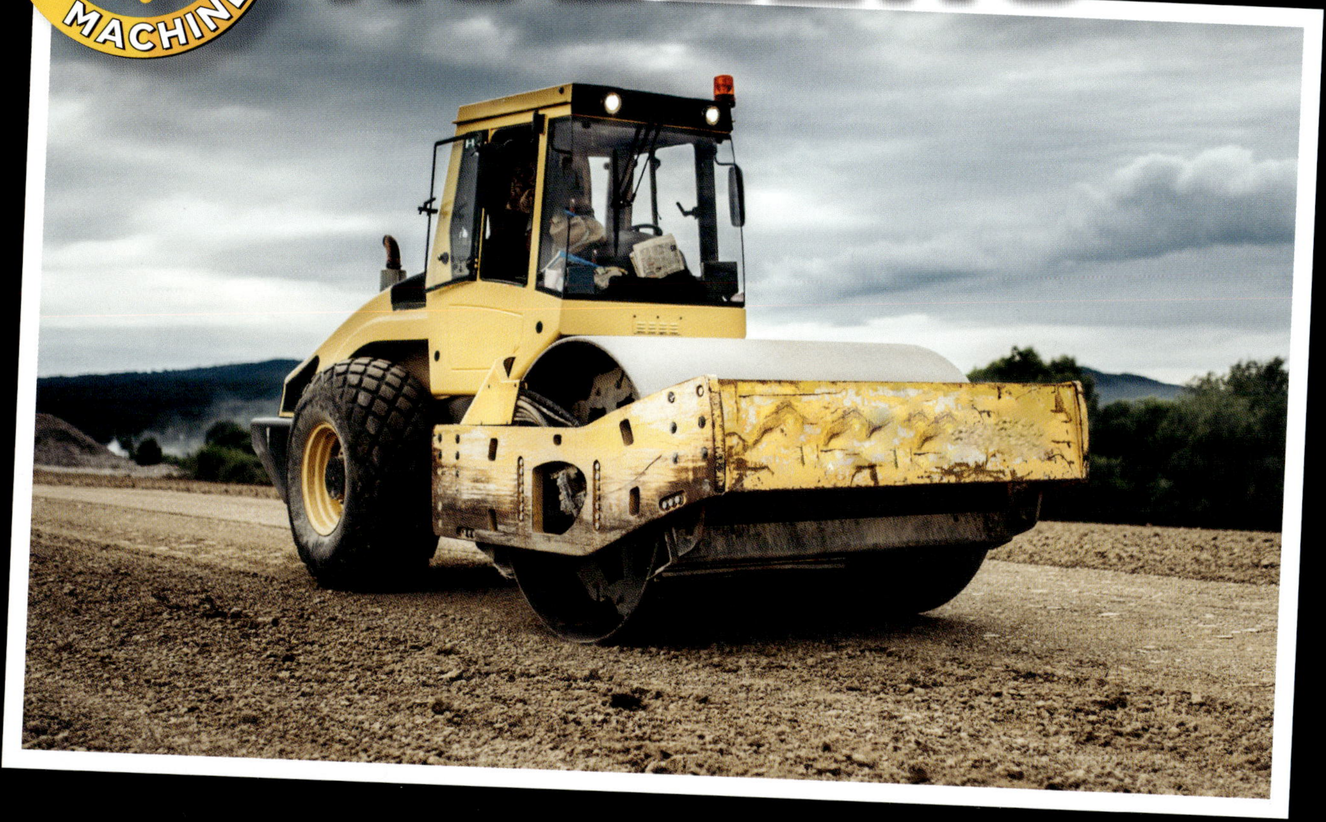

Mitchell Lane
PUBLISHERS

2001 SW 31st Avenue
Hallandale, FL 33009
www.mitchelllane.com

First Edition, 2021.

Author: Paul Zachary
Designer: Ed Morgan
Editor: Morgan Brody

Little Mitchie is an imprint of Mitchell Lane Publishers.

Title: Construction Machines: Road Rollers / by Paul Zachary
Description: Hallandale, FL :
Mitchell Lane Publishers, [2021]

Series: Construction Machines
Library bound ISBN: 978-1-68020-692-0
eBook ISBN: 978-1-68020-693-7

Photo credits: Shutterstock, freepik.com

CONTENTS

Words in **bold** can be found in the Glossary.

Rollin' Rollin' Rollin'
Here comes the road roller!

The road roller is at the **construction site**. It helps to build roads.

The road roller **compacts** soil, gravel, concrete or **asphalt**. The roller is the key to getting the **smoothest** surface.

asphalt
roller

First the road roller rolls over the soil or gravel. Then the asphalt is poured and the roller presses the asphalt into place.

Road rollers have large steel **drums**.

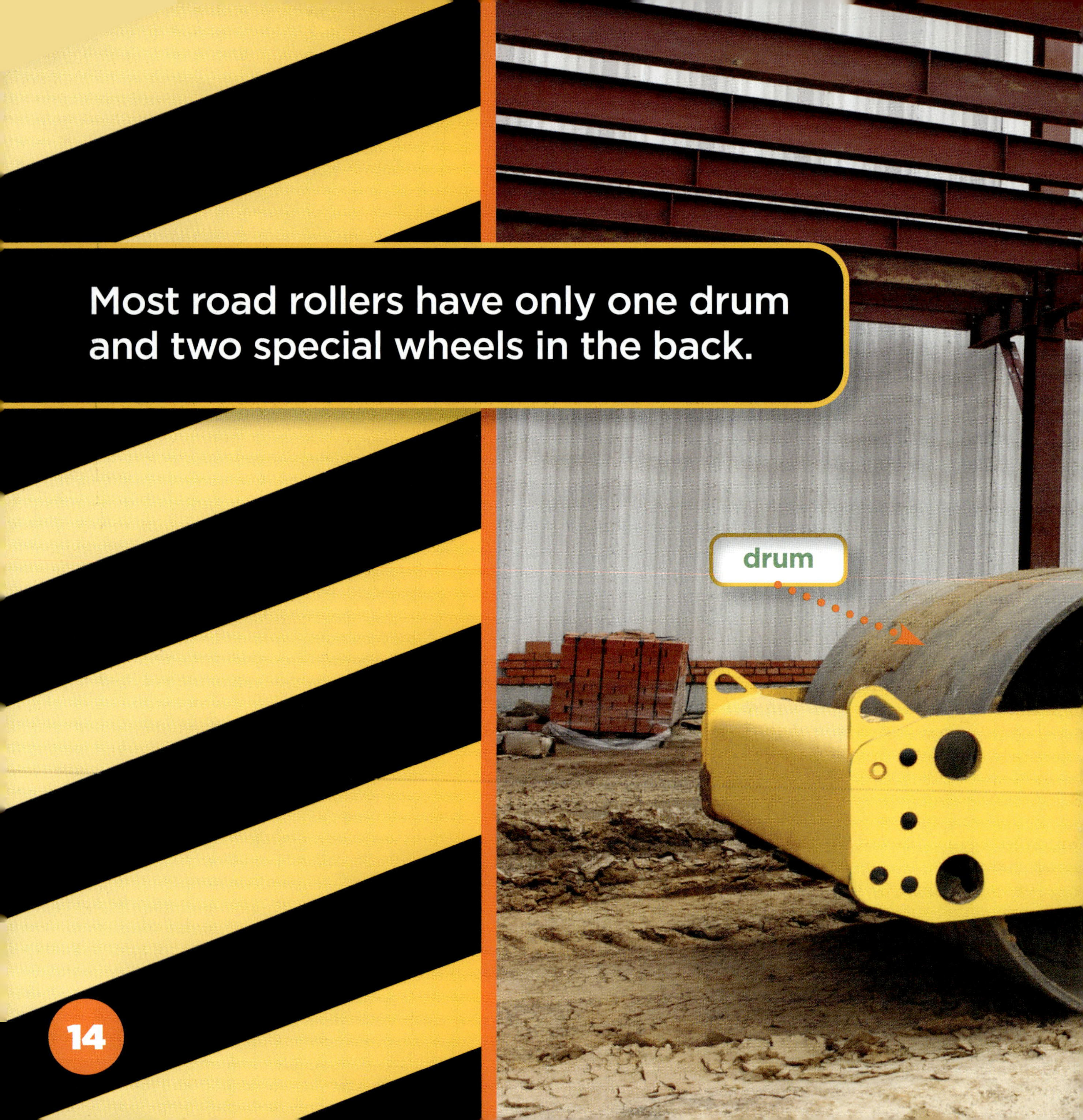

Most road rollers have only one drum and two special wheels in the back.

wheel

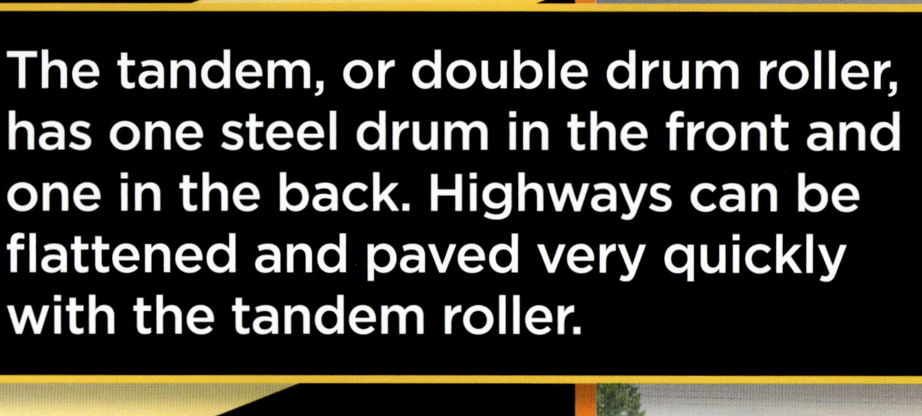

The tandem, or double drum roller, has one steel drum in the front and one in the back. Highways can be flattened and paved very quickly with the tandem roller.

cab

The driver sits in the **cab**.
The driver **operates** the road roller.

The road roller is very important at the construction site.

INTERESTING FACTS

- The first road rollers were pulled by oxen and horses.
- Next came rollers that were powered by steam.
- Today's rollers run on **diesel fuel**.
- Steamrollers have been popular in movies, music and books, including the *Thomas the Tank Engine and Friends* series and *Bob the Builder* episodes.

GLOSSARY

asphalt
A thick, black, tar-like liquid used for making roads

cab
The part of the road roller where the driver sits

compact
To press something so it fills less space and becomes harder

construction site
Place where things are built

diesel fuel
A type of fuel that is used in vehicles with diesel engines

drum
Big, round rollers at the bottom of the road roller

operator
The person who works a machine

smooth
Soft and even, without any bumps

SOURCES

What is a Road Roller. 2019.

*Rick the Road Roller and More Trucks for Childre*n. 2017.

Squishing Fruit with Rick the Road Roller. 2018.

FURTHER READING

Bell, Samantha. *Road Roller*. North Mankato, MN: Cherry Lake Publishers, 2019.

INDEX

ABOUT THE AUTHOR

PAUL ZACHARY has recently moved into a new community. He is fascinated by all the construction machines used to build streets, sidewalks, new homes, and even tennis courts. Watching the road roller at work was particularly exciting because that meant the roads were finally smooth enough to drive on.